I0683393

Waiting Tables?
Make More Money!

By Dan Longton

Copyright © 2024: Dan Longton
All Rights Reserved. ISBN: 979-8-89324-330-7
Printed in the United States of America.

No part of this publication shall be reproduced, transmitted, or sold in whole or in part in any form without prior written consent of the author, except as provided by the United States of America copyright law. Any unauthorized usage of the text without express written permission of the publisher is a violation of the author's copyright and is illegal and punishable by law. all trademarks and registered trademarks appearing in this guide are the property of their respective owners.

The opinions expressed by the author are not necessarily those held Publishers.

The information contained within this book is strictly for informational purposes. the material may include information, products, or services by third parties. As such, the author and publisher do not assume responsibility or liability for any third-party material or opinions. the publisher is not responsible for websites (or their content) that are not owned by the publisher. readers are advised to do their own due diligence when it comes to making decisions.

Acknowledgment:

Thanks to the millions of Waitpersons who serve customers every day creating ENTHUSIASTIC experiences. You are valued and deserve to Make More Money!

Dedication

My family for their love and support!
Christine Bliss Wife
Lauren Artist Daughter
Miguel Son
Dr. Wallace A Longton MD Brother
Burtice M Longton, Mom

Table Of Contents

Waiting Tables?
Make More MONEY!

Welcome to a rewarding and enjoyable learning experience.

Use of this guide will help you Make More Money!

You will learn easy and enjoyable techniques to increase customers' ENTHUSIASM for their dining experience. In return for your thoughtfulness and performance, you will be rewarded with more TIP income. You, restaurant owners and managers, will benefit from more repeat business.

You will enjoy increased TIP income as you implement the skills and techniques you learn from "Waiting Tables? Make More Money!"

Introduction to Waiting Tables?
Make More Money!

Research shows that well-trained waitpersons earn more money for themselves from ENTHUSIASTIC CUSTOMERS.

It was developed from extensive interviews with restaurant customers discussing what types of service motivate them to ENTHUSIASTICALLY reward servers with bigger TIPS.

1

What will "Waiting Tables? Make More Money!" do for you?

It will provide knowledge and skills to help you improve your restaurant selling resulting in:

Higher-income through better selling during the four phases of the restaurant sales cycle:

More satisfied and enthusiastic customers who will:

Order more and TIP more.

Treat you better.

Return to your restaurant and, on many occasions, ask for you personally.

Refer the restaurant to their friends and family.

 *Exercise:*

Write what would you do with the additional income if you increased your TIP earnings by 10 to 25%?

_____

_____

_____

_____

_____

_____

How to use "Waiting Tables? Make More Money!"

Exercises are included to increase learning and retention. Complete the exercises as you progress through each chapter.

THE WAITPERSON'S JOB

An Important Job

Waitpersons are the primary contact the customer has with your restaurant. You ensure that the customer has an ENTHUSIASTIC dining experience.

The way you do your job will determine the customer's perception of the restaurant, including the food taste, ambiance, seating, and overall experience.

The Waitperson is a Commissioned Salesperson

Waitpersons who consider themselves commissioned salespeople will be more successful. Commissioned salespeople understand that ENTHUSIASTIC customers purchase more and are more concerned that their salespeople are well rewarded.

Increase Commission

A waitperson has advantages over many sales positions. Most sales jobs have a fixed commission rate. You can raise your tip commission percentage.

Controlling your Destiny and Income

You have the power and ability to be a success. It is your choice.

You control your destiny by acquiring the skills and knowledge needed to promote customer enjoyment and satisfaction. Use the techniques you learn from "Waiting Tables? Make More Money!" and you will be on your way to bigger TIPS!

The Waitperson TIP Income Formula Is:

TIPS = Meal Size ($) X Customer ENTHUSIASM (TIP percentage)

This simple formula provides earning power for you with every customer served.

Remember these SIX words:

"TIPS come from Customer ENTHUSIASM.... Period!

Treat each customer in a manner to increase their ENTHUSIASM and Make More Money!

Meal Size

Meal Size is the total dollar value of the meal before TIP. You will increase your TIP by increasing the meal size. You should recommend Meal Enhancers, including before-dinner drinks, appetizers, and desserts.

Recommend the Meal Enhancers appropriate for your specific customer. It is important to make recommendations in a thoughtful manner. Do not appear to be pushing items for the sake of inflating the meal size.

Customers have their own reasons for dining. Only they know how much they can afford to spend. Polite Meal Enhancer recommendations will be well received by your customers.

Attitude

Who makes the difference? You do! That is right, you! The most important person in your work life is you. Successful selling depends heavily upon attitude. Waitpersons sell themselves first and meals second.

Who would want to go to a restaurant with great food but crabby or grumpy or inefficient waitpersons? Not many, and probably not you. On the other hand, restaurants with smiling and efficient waitpersons are busy even if the food is not superior. Why? Because the waitperson makes the difference.

Your attitude is the way you feel about yourself, your work and others. When you feel good about yourself, others sense it, and they feel good. If you truly like people, it will be easy to smile and be friendly. Customers like waitpersons with a positive attitude.

Positively People Attitude

The best waitperson attitude is a **"POSITIVELY PEOPLE"** attitude. You have a **"POSITIVELY PEOPLE"** attitude when you feel great about yourself, your customers, and the opportunity to add happiness to their lives.

Show off your **POSITIVELY PEOPLE** attitude to customers. You can be proud of yourself as a waitperson who earns TIP income in a great restaurant. Let your pride shine through to everyone you meet at work, and you will be rewarded with bigger TIPS from ENTHUSIASTIC customers.

✏️ *Exercise:*

Take a moment to think about yourself. Jot down five things that make you feel good and contribute to a positive attitude.

———————————————————————

———————————————————————

———————————————————————

———————————————————————

———————————————————————

✏️ *Exercise:*

Think about the positive traits or behaviors of customers and jot down five things you appreciate about them.

_____

_____

_____

_____

_____

_____

Customer ENTHUSIASM Value to YOU...Do the Math

Remember that customer ENTHUSIASM is the most important factor in the Waitperson Income Formula. Waitpersons must make it their primary responsibility. You will generate greater TIP income if every action you take improves customer enthusiasm. For example, consider:

A customer Meal Size is $20.00. The customer frequently tips 10 percent. A $8.00 meal enhancer, such as a shared dessert, will increase the meal size to $28.00. Your tip will increase by $0.80.

If you increase Customer ENTHUSIASM the customer will probably increase the TIP percentage by 5 or 10 percent. The extra 5 percent will provide an additional $1.40, and the extra 10 percent will provide you with $2.80 more tip income.

The Restaurant Sales Cycle

The Restaurant Sales Cycle is the normal customer visit flow. It has four distinct and important phases: Greeting, Ordering, Feeding, and Fleeting. Each phase must be managed to produce maximum customer ENTHUSIASM.

GREETING begins the moment a customer enters the restaurant. Customers build their first and often most enduring impression in this phase. The Greeting includes a meeting, seating, and a Waitperson introduction.

ORDERING begins with the Waitperson Introduction and includes the Menu presentation, Specials explanations and Customer Order taking.

FEEDING is the delivery of all customer order items, including Special Requests, Meal Enhancers and being Attentive and Accessible.

FLEETING begins with customer bill readiness and ends with the customer's departure.

THE GREETING

The Greeting portion of the Restaurant sales cycle begins the moment the customer enters the Restaurant and is completed when the Waitperson takes the first order.

Readiness Questions ❓

Review the following questions for Chapter readiness.

What are the three stages of the GREETING? What is the purpose of the first greeting?

Do actions consist of statements, questions, answers, and deliverables?

Should Waitpersons introduce themselves by name?

What two things must be determined by assessing the Customer during the GREETING?

The Greeting itself often consists of three stages:

First Greeting

Seating Greeting

Waitperson Introduction.

Usually, the customer's first contact with the restaurant staff is by the hostess or host. The initial greeting should create a positive customer impression that will enhance their dining experience.

First Greeting

The First Greeting includes meeting and seating the customer.

The person performing the GREETING will usually provide menus to the customers when seating them.

SQAD

The Waitperson's key to success is performing the proper action at the right time. Actions consist of **Statements, Questions, Answers and Deliverables** (Use the initials "SQAD" to help your memory). Customer enthusiasm depends upon your actions being:

Timely - the customer will be most satisfied with the appropriate action done quickly.

Supported by the proper body language, expression, and tone of voice.

Customer-focused - every customer wants to feel that the restaurant is very glad to have them as a customer.

The following are examples of Statements:

"Welcome."

"We are glad you chose us today."

"The Beef Wellington is excellent."

Questions should determine customers' preferences. Examples:

"Are you ready for drinks?"

"May I show you our delicious desserts?"

Customer answers to your questions are important because they indicate preferences. Deliverables are responses to answers and must reflect customer preferences. They include the items you bring to the table and actions on behalf of the customer, including order-taking and food serving.

The Seating Greeting

The first person to meet your customer after the customer is seated provides the seating greeting. Your restaurant may have a water and cocktail server who greets the customer at your table, supplies water and takes the initial drink order. Always remember that the customer is your customer, the source of your income. Therefore, you will want to make certain that this phase of the Greeting is managed properly. Scanning your tables will provide you with information to make that judgment. If quality customer treatment does not occur, you will need to take particular care with your customer including interventions such as taking the drink order yourself. In many restaurants the Waitperson delivers the seating greeting with the waitperson introduction. In such restaurants, the quality of the seating greeting is controlled by the Waitperson.

Waitperson Introduction

The Waitperson Introduction may be your first contact with the customer. You must introduce yourself as soon as possible.

TWO Minute Seating Rule:

Introduce yourself to the customer within two minutes after seating.

It is common knowledge that people are strongly influenced by first impressions. Therefore, the timeliness and quality of your introduction will influence the customer's impression of you and your restaurant for the remainder of the restaurant's selling cycle. Delay of the Seating Greeting will diminish the quality of the greeting and can lower TIP income significantly.

The Waitperson introduction

Customer greeting.

Customers seat themselves in many restaurants. The Waitperson is then the first to greet them. Be sure to greet each customer as you would a friend and guest to your home. This will ensure that the customer's first impression is positive.

Assess the customer.

You should determine customer preferences from direct questions and observations about their:

Dining Reasons
Time Available
General Mood

✏️ *Exercise:*

Think about the first things you'd like to know from customers. Write down two questions that you'd ask them initially to understand their preferences.

_____

_____

_____

_____

_____

An Introduction Example:

"Hello, my name is Kelly, and I'm your Waitperson (waiter or waitress). I will do my very best to provide you with excellent service. Please let me know if you have any special preferences or are on a tight schedule. May I get you something to drink?"

The introduction example includes a question regarding customer preferences. Remember that understanding the customer and the customer's preference should be ongoing throughout the restaurant sales cycle. In sum, you should continuously uncover:

✏️ *Exercise:*

Pen down an introduction that feels just right to you. It's the one you'd confidently use to introduce yourself.

THE ORDERING

ORDERING begins after the Greeting when the Waitperson begins to take a drink order or present the menu. ORDERING is the primary selection process. Additional items will continue to be ordered, like drink refills and dessert. You must handle the initial order as a special phase in the Waitperson Sales Cycle. ORDERING is the business aspect of a Customer's dining experience. During Ordering the Waitperson must consider the Customers dominant B-E-S-T personality style and the reason for dining.

Ordering creates expectations in the customer's mind that they will be happy with what arrives as a result of the order.

WHAT and WHEN

The Waitperson must manage the Customer's expectations with regard to WHAT will arrive and WHEN it will be served.

Ordering requires a complete knowledge of your restaurant's menu selections and how to talk about them to the customer. This requires some effort on your part to prepare yourself thoroughly.

Readiness Questions ❓

Which order must be taken fast?
Should you recommend the highest-priced selection?
What two customers' expectations are managed during Ordering?

What are the two kinds of special requests?
Should the Waitperson repeat special requests back to the Customer to ensure understanding? Ordering rule number 1

Ordering Expectation Rule

FIRST Order FAST

After the Greeting, it is important to offer to take the first order as soon as possible. This can be an offer to take a drink order or an appetizer order. It is appropriate to say, "Would you like to start with drinks or appetizers?"

Taking the First order FAST will relax your customers as they take any time needed to examine the menu.

At the time of the First order FAST, your customer should be presented with the menu if the First Greeting person did not provide it.

When customers order drinks, delivery is expected **the next time they see you**. If the drinks order takes longer than three to five minutes, visit the Customer and advise,

"Your drinks are being prepared and will be right up." You manage and reset the customer's expectations, plus the additional attention will help defray potential dissatisfaction. It also demonstrates that you care about the customer.

This additional visit will give your Customer a chance to ask you any questions about the menu and place an appetizer order.

Menu Explanations

Your Customers will vary on the amount of explanation they require.

If your management requires you to present daily specials, you must decide whether or not your Customer wants the specials list described in detail. If the daily specials are a written list for the Customer, ask, "May I review our daily Specials for you?" Then, gauge the Customer's response. The Engineer type may want to analyze the written special list. The Thinker may want more detail about every item, while the Socializer may want to know which items people seem to enjoy the most.

After you have served any drinks or appetizers and your Customer has had time to examine the menu ask, "May I explain any of our menu items for you?"

If your Customer answers, "Yes." Explain each item briefly. If your Customer indicates no, suggest, "May I allow you time to consider your choices, or are you ready to place your order?"

As with daily specials, allow the customer to direct your next action. Read Customers' signals to determine how much information to provide beyond what can be read. You will be most successful if you give customers enough information to meet their requirements.

Making Recommendations

When asked to make a recommendation, DO NOT recommend the most expensive items on the menu. Customers are sensitive to prices and usually perceive attempts to "up the bill" with recommendations. You should ask questions to guide you to appropriate suggestions. Ask questions such as:

"Do you prefer Beef, Poultry, Fish or Pasta?

Your questions will help customers narrow their choices. Their answers will indicate the type of selections that you should recommend.

 *Exercise:*

Think about how you'd guide customers toward the best choices. Write down two questions you'd ask to assist you in making personalized recommendations.

Your recommendation should include the name of the dish and a positive statement such as:

"The Veal Parmesan looks excellent tonight."

_____

_____

_____

_____

_____

_____

✏️ *Exercise:*

Consider the best advice you can offer. Write down four recommendations along with a positive statement for each, highlighting why it's a great choice.

_____

_____

_____

_____

_____

Customer Order Expectations

The two Customer Order Expectations groups are:

WHAT and WHEN

WHAT will arrive is important to Customer Enthusiasm. During ORDERING, your Customer will establish a mental picture of **WHAT** they are ordering. The Waitperson is responsible for ensuring that customers have information to correctly visualize **WHAT** will arrive at the table. The actions of questioning and answering provide that information.

Preparation questions are needed for many menu selections. You should simply ask questions, including:

"How would you like your eggs prepared?""How would you like your steak prepared?"
"Do you prefer your salad dressing on the side?"
"Would you prefer white, wheat or rye bread?"

You should also ask questions that provide you with information regarding customers' desired meal sizes. Customers who inform you that they are very hungry should be advised which meals have large portions. Otherwise, customers expecting a large meal may be served a small meal.

 *Exercise:*

Think about the menu items you'd like to highlight. Jot down two menu selections along with a question about their preparation for each dish.

Menu Information should be clearly and accurately stated to help customers understand just WHAT they are ordering. Examples of information statements are:

"Medium rare in our restaurant is prepared slightly pink."

"The Cajun seasoning is a bit spicy."

"The steak Diana is prepared at your table."

 ### *Exercise:*

Consider the details that would enhance understanding of menu selections. List four menu items along with examples of relevant facts and clarifying information for each dish.

_____

_____

_____

_____

_____

_____

The second **ORDERING RULE** is:

"SAY WHEN the ordered items will arrive."

We are all conditioned to expect our requests and desires to be fulfilled very rapidly. Drive-through hamburgers, automatic bank tellers and even situation comedies promote instant gratification and solutions. It is important to remember that most customers have PRESET EXPECTATIONS that WHEN will be very fast. This expectation carries over even to more relaxed settings. Therefore, it is advisable to error on the rapid side rather than the slow. Better yet, determine your customers' WHEN expectations and meet them. Advise your customers of the meal preparation progress, especially those who appear impatient or whose meal preparation is longer than expected. SCANNING your tables will provide you with continuous input.

Customers' **WHEN EXPECTATIONS** can best be managed through communication: 1) advise the Chef or kitchen manager that you have a customer on a tight schedule, and 2) continual contact with the customers will allow you to reset expectations in small steps before dissatisfaction occurs. If you are busy serving several tables and must deliver a drink order to the bar before taking an order from another customer, advise the customer, "I'll be back in a moment to take your drink order." When food preparation is longer than customers' expectations, communicate the causes when known and advise when the meal will be ready.

Examples of **SAY WHEN** communication include:

"Your order is being carefully prepared now and will be ready in a few minutes," or "The Chef is very busy carefully preparing each order. It is taking a bit longer than normal and will be ready in a few minutes."

Expectation Management

The ONLY reason a person becomes upset is their expectations are missed.

Meet and exceed customer expectations to increase ENTHUSIASM and Make More Money!

Waitpersons have little influence over food preparation times. Apart from special requests to the Chef, your primary role on the restaurant team is CUSTOMER EXPECTATIONS management. Communication is your primary expectation management tool.

The steps of expectation management are:
Determine preset expectations.
Reset preset expectations where necessary.
Set expectations according to customer choices.
Reset expectations in small steps when necessary.
Meet expectations whenever possible.

It is a challenge for waitpersons to know all of their customers' many PRESET EXPECTATIONS. However, through customer communication, you can understand their most important preset expectations and then manage those expectations.

By communicating with your customers you SET EXPECTATIONS and RESET EXPECTATIONS. After setting CUSTOMER EXPECTATIONS, they will be enthusiastic when expectations are met and not satisfied when expectations are missed. You are successful when you

27

properly SET CUSTOMER EXPECTATIONS and deliver to those expectations.

Customers TIP more when their EXPECTATIONS are met or exceeded!

Ordering Rule Number 3

Special request - Pass the test!

Special requests are excellent opportunities for Waitpersons to improve Customer Enthusiasm.

There are two kinds of SPECIAL REQUESTS:

Can Do and Cannot Do.

The Waitperson will frequently know whether a SPECIAL REQUEST can be met. Sometimes, the Waitperson must check with restaurant management or the Chef to determine if a SPECIAL REQUEST can be fulfilled and, if so, whether it will require additional charges.

Approach a SPECIAL REQUEST as an impromptu test given by the Customer. PASS THE TEST by meeting the SPECIAL REQUEST or providing an acceptable alternative to Customers.

Health-Related Special Requests

Doctors and Dietitians have determined that many food additives and many foods contain chemicals that should be avoided by many people. Some of these people are your customers. They will usually ask for special preparation to avoid the chemicals. Some may only provide a signal to you by asking if the food is prepared using additives such as salt, spices, iodine, or monosodium glutamate (called MSG).

You should respond to health-related special requests with care and accuracy. Some of your customers may be sensitive enough to such chemicals to become critically ill after consuming them.

You will also be asked for items that are acceptable for special diets, such as heart smart or diabetes.

Some may request a substitute for cream sauce or butter to avoid fat and cholesterol. Other customers with special dental work, such as dentures, will have difficulty chewing fibrous or hard foods.

✏️ *Exercise:*

Think about special requests and how you can accommodate them from your menu. Write down two recommendations tailored to a specific special request category.

_____

_____

_____

_____

_____

_____

View SPECIAL REQUESTS as a test and it will be easier to cheerfully help customers with medical or special diet needs.

You can fulfill special requests with accuracy only if you clearly hear and understand them. Repeat SPECIAL REQUESTS back to your customers and then ask, "Is that correct?" Where necessary, ask for further clarification.

Example of a customer special request: **"Can you prepare the grilled chicken without MSG?"**

If a Customer asks if they can substitute a vegetable for the salad, respond, "Would you like the green beans vegetable in place of the salad, is that correct?"

After clarification, set customers' expectations for "can do" SPECIAL REQUESTS by saying, "Yes, we will be happy to." You will make the customer feel good and set expectations that their SPECIAL REQUESTS will be achieved.

Note: be sure to verify that the preparation of the SPECIAL REQUEST was correct before serving the order. When serving, say, "Your order was prepared as you requested," then repeat the special request, for example, "without the MSG."

Set the Customer expectations for SPECIAL REQUESTS fulfillment of which you are uncertain by saying. "I am not certain if this is possible. Please allow me to check with the Chef (or Manager) and I'll be right back with you."

If there is a charge for the substitution or special preparation, communicate to the customer, "There is a nominal charge of $ (state the amount), would you like us to go ahead for you?"

If the SPECIAL REQUEST cannot be done, promptly communicate to your customer, "I am sorry, but we are unable to accomplish your request because... (state a reason)." The Customer will probably be disappointed but will feel better if there is a good reason, such as, "the MSG is added ahead of time." Be certain to indicate any menu items that do not have MSG, even if not the customer's preferred choice. Then, ask the Customer, "Would you like some time to review the menu for another selection?"

✏️ *Exercise:*

Consider the special requests that customers might make and how your restaurant handles them. List two special requests along with your restaurant's policy for each, and write down what you would say to customers making those requests.

_____

_____

_____

_____

_____

_____

Menu Collection

Collect menus from each customer following their order. However, be sensitive to a customer wishing to continue to review it in case they are considering adding something.

Chapter Summary

ORDERING is the actual business transaction phase of the Restaurant Sales Cycle. During ORDERING, the Waitperson sets Customer Expectations for the food to be served. The two primary expectations to manage are WHAT and WHEN.

Give Customers enough information to make informed decisions about WHAT they are ORDERING. Ask preference-seeking questions to assist with your recommendations. Treat Special Requests as opportunities to PASS THE TEST that will result in larger tips.

The Feeding

FEEDING begins when the order is served and ends when customers are ready for their checks. It includes serving food, table clearing and follow-on orders such as dessert and after-dinner drinks. Waitpersons need to frequently SCAN and visit their tables during the FEEDING phase to ensure customer enthusiasm. During FEEDING, waitpersons are performers. Successful performers anticipate needs and frequently deliver to needs before asked.

Readiness Questions ❓

Review the following questions for Chapter preparation.

Is it better to anticipate customer needs before you are asked?

How do you remember who orders what?

When do you want to be a GHOST Waitperson?

What two things begin with the letter A for which customers say they will TIP more?

How can you be Accessible to your guests?

Customer's expectations during FEEDING must be met. They include receiving a correct order that has been properly prepared. Therefore, double-check each order prior to serving to ensure that it is correct and prepared properly. Also, be certain that Hot foods are Hot and Cold foods are Cold. Give the same consideration to your customer as you would a home dinner guest with a meal you personally prepared. Pay particular attention to Special Requests, and be sure to mention to your guest that the Special Request was accommodated.

Customers expect you to remember what they order. It may help to take orders in a clockwise direction around the table and make a mental note of where you started. Memorization techniques are especially important if your restaurant requires you to memorize orders. Order mix ups are like calling a person by the wrong name and can make you appear uninterested and ineffective. On the other hand, customers are usually impressed when waitpersons remember multiple food orders.

✏️ *Exercise:*

Write down your method of remembering Special Requests and what each Guest ordered.

_____

_____

_____

_____

_____

As you serve the order, check that your customers have the right accompaniments, i.e., butter, salt, or sour cream. If you notice something needed, tell the Customers that you will be right back with the item. Also, inquire whether anything else is needed, "May I bring anything else for you at this time?" Never make customers wait for condiments or other food accompaniments. Dissatisfaction rapidly increases when people have their food but not the pepper or catsup their taste requires.

During FEEDING, customers need their expectations met quickly to fully enjoy their meal.

Questioning

Allow your guest a few minutes to begin eating. Then follow up with this question:

"Is everything prepared to your satisfaction?"

Most Customers will answer "yes." But, when they indicate otherwise, immediately correct the situation. Neither debate nor try to convince them that their concerns are not real. Suggest a solution that sets expectations, then PERFORM accordingly.

Examples include under and over-cooked steaks. If your customer thinks the steak is undercooked, ask:

"Would you like your steak cooked a little longer?"

If the steak is overcooked, ask:

"Would you like another steak prepared for you? We would be happy to."

Avoid asking questions when customers are chewing their food. Simply wait for them to swallow, then ask the question.

GHOSTING

You are GHOSTING when you fulfill customers' needs without their conscious awareness of your actions. GHOSTING is very effective during the feeding portion of the sales cycle - when customers are concentrating on their meal and their companions.

Quietly take care of your guests' needs; refill water glasses and bread baskets. Remove used dishes and flatware. It is important that you follow up with refills and removal of used dishes during FEEDING.

 *Exercise:*

Consider subtle ways to attend to customers' needs without drawing attention. List two actions you can take when employing the technique of 'ghosting' during the feeding phase of the sales cycle.

_____

_____

_____

_____

D-A-N-C-E

Remember the acronym D-A-N-C-E during the FEEDING. It will help you remember the key actions that produce customer ENTHUSIASM.

Do Anticipate Next Customer Expectations

The two key actions of the D-A-N-C-E performance are to be:

Attentive
Accessible

You want to use your senses to SEE and HEAR clues that will let you know what customers need before they ask.

Our surveys asked customers to state the key Waitperson behaviors that will cause them to TIP more.

Most responded being **ATTENTIVE** and **ACCESSIBLE** as the key behaviors.

Be attentive by visiting your quests as frequently as possible. But, interrupt conversation only for a good reason. Your GHOSTING techniques to be a PEAK PERFORMER and to avoid unnecessary interruptions.

Your frequent visits or scans will help you maximize ACCESSIBILITY. Customers, particularly the elderly, become frustrated and dissatisfied if they cannot get the attention of their Waitperson. Use brief eye contact on a GHOSTING visit or a scan; customers who wish to speak to you will respond to your eye contact.

MEAL ENHANCERS

Visit your customers' tables when they have nearly completed the main order and ask if they would care for coffee, dessert, or other meal enhancers.

Meal enhancers are important for restaurant profit and your TIP income. However, you must not appear to be pushing enhancers, only increase the meal price. Allow your customers to make the decisions with your gentle urging. Many restaurants use a dessert tray to compliment your efforts.

Approach your guests with the dessert tray and ask, for example:

"May I show you our dessert tray?" or

"Would you care to see our delicious dessert assortment?"

If your Guest says "no." Respond with "Thank you.." If they say "No, thank you." Respond with "You are welcome."

Most customers will agree to see deserts. Show them the tray by pointing out each dessert. Provide a positive description using words such as:

Fresh raspberries
Delightful white chocolate
Rich dark chocolate

Delicious strawberries

Low-calorie or low-fat desserts

You should recommend available lite dessert (low fat, low calorie or not very filling) selections to customers who express that they are full. Saying something such as:

"Our low-calorie sherbet with nonfat topping is very light and refreshing."

✏️ *Exercise:*

List two desserts along with the descriptions you'll use to highlight their appeal.

_____

_____

_____

_____

_____

Customers will often be willing to share a dessert. So, when you notice one person tempted by the dessert and the others not, suggest, "Would you care to share the (name of dessert)?" You may add, when appropriate, "I can bring it on two plates."

If customers decide to share desserts, remember to bring additional silverware and plates.

CLEAN UP

Guests relax and feel more comfortable when used dishes and utensils are removed. Scan frequently to see if customers have completed the use of dishes. You may use your peak performance GHOSTING technique to remove them from the table.

Also, remove general disposable items such as:

empty sugar packets
used coffee cream unit cups
soiled paper napkins
cracker wrappers.

Remember to anticipate guest needs and replenish accompaniments if needed. Also, replenish clean paper napkins.

An example of good clean-up action where you D-A-N-C-E is:

A Guest is drinking coffee, and you clear coffee cream unit cups. Use Ghosting and serve replacement coffee cream units before your Guest asks.

Chapter Summary

Treat your customers as personal guests during the FEEDING Sales Cycle Phase. Set and Fulfill their meal expectations in the same way. Meal expectations include providing the right order to the right person and delivering all of the appropriate condiments and accessories. Enthusiasm increases as you "**D**o **A**nticipate **N**ext **C**ustomer **E**xpectations" (D-A-N-C-E) and meet their needs before being asked to. Waitpersons must be Attentive and Accessible to successfully anticipate expectations.

GHOSTING is a technique whereby you can take care of customers without interruptions.

Frequent customer visits, scans, return visits and quick responses during FEEDING add to your customers' dining enthusiasm.

The Fleeting

The final phase of the restaurant sales cycle is termed FLEETING for good reason. Today's customers are busy. Our society is fast-paced. Customers are usually ready for a quick departure when they reach what they decide is the end of their dining experience. Your job at this point is to smoothly and pleasantly help them depart.

The Fleeting cycle begins when the customer has finished eating, including dessert and after-dinner drinks. You can continue to improve customer ENTHUSIASM or undo much of the good work you have done.

The Fleeting consists of three parts: Bill Readiness, Bill Presentation and Bill Returning. Each part has the potential for you to avoid a delay. Be aware that delays and satisfaction are defined by customers. Make certain the customer is neither hurried nor delayed during any part of the Fleeting.

Consider the following readiness questions: ?

Customers who take a long time to eat are never in a hurry for their bill, true or false.

Since FLEETING is at the end of the meal what should be done for final customer satisfaction?

What are the three parts of FLEETING?

How do you set Customer expectations about bill readiness?

Is it a promising idea to present your customer with mints at a bill presentation?

Bill Readiness

Customers frequently have a good dining experience spoiled by a long wait to receive their bill. This occurs despite body language, hand signals and other attention-gaining maneuvers by the Customer to gain access to the Waitperson. All too often customers have to leave their table to track down the Waitperson or another person just to get the bill. All the good work during the restaurant sales cycle may be lost. This delay frequently results in dissatisfaction and tip reduction. TIP dollars can diminish as much as 1/2 if waiting is beyond expectations.

Fleeting Rule

When customers are DONE, they are ready to RUN!

There are several things to do to ensure Customers do not wait too long:

Even when the customer has taken a long time to consume the meal the Waitperson must assume that the customer does care how long it takes to get his/her bill.

When the Waitperson is busy with new customers, adopt the attitude that the customer "will not have to wait to get their bill."

Restaurant bill preparation should be done before the Customer asks for it.

The Waitperson should observe when customers finish consuming their meal or after dinner desserts and drinks. All of your tables should be scanned regularly.

But again, do not assume - customers whose dining has been leisurely are not ready to go fast when they have finished the meal. It is your job to make every customer's "FLEETING" timely.

 *Exercise:*

Picture a customer who's likely to eat quickly and leave soon after. Describe what this type of customer might be like.

_____

_____

_____

_____

Bill Readiness Questions ❓

When your customer appears finished, simply ask, "Would you like your check now, or is there something else I can get for you." Don't hesitate to make further suggestions unless it is obvious that the customer has become impatient. But remember to not over-press for meal enhancers.

Do your best, however, to make the bill presentation timely. But, if the customer is ready for the bill and you know that the bill preparation will take longer than desirable, set the customer's expectations that it will take a little longer than usual. " I'll do my best to get the bill to you right away."

Food To Go

Customers may wish to take home unfinished portions of their meal. When you notice that a portion is remaining, ask: "Would you like your _____ TO GO?"

The two ways of preparing food TO GO are to provide a container for the customer to fill or by taking the plate and preparing it for them.

✏️ *Exercise:*

Consider how your restaurant handles requests for taking leftover food home. Write down the method your restaurant uses for preparing TO GO portions: do you remove food from the table and package it, or do you let customers pack their own?

_____

_____

_____

_____

_____

_____

Bill Presentation

As mentioned, time the Bill Presentation to the customers' expectations. Courteously present the bill to customers or, in some cases, to "the tables." Do not drop the bill and immediately leave. You should present the bill with a tentative close, such as:

"We really appreciate your business. Is there anything else I can get for you?"

"I've enjoyed serving you. Please come again. Would you like anything else - more coffee?."
Please ask for me again and I'll make certain you receive special care.

 *Exercise:*

Consider the polite and courteous phrases you'll use when presenting the bill to customers. Write down what you will say to customers during the bill presentation.

_____

_____

_____

_____

_____

_____

Departing Comments

It is important to extend your customers a pleasant farewell when you see them leaving, such as:

"I have enjoyed serving you, please come back soon," or "Thank you, and have a pleasant evening."

 ### *Exercise:*

Consider the polite and pleasant remarks you'll use when customers are leaving your establishment. Write down what you will say as your departing comments to customers.

_____

_____

_____

_____

_____

_____

Chapter Summary

FLEETING is a perfect term to describe Customers' readiness to leave after a meal is finished. Even Customers who eat leisurely are ready to FLEET quickly when they have finished their meal.

The three parts of fleeting are Bill Readiness, presenting the bill and returning the bill. It is important to thank your Customers at the final bill presentation and as they are leaving the table.

SPECIAL CUSTOMER SITUATIONS

Many special customer situations will occur, including difficult or inebriated customers, those who refuse food, and troublesome children. Use your best judgment when these occur and involve your Manager where appropriate.

Remember, the important goal is to satisfy reasonable customer requests. If you are not sure of the reasonableness, then escalate the situation immediately to your Manager. Managers want satisfied Customers and will be glad to help. If needed most will discuss the requests table side with your customers.

Four Techniques will help when Special Customer Situations arise:

Extra Courtesies
Appropriate responses
Problem reducers
Escalation

Chapter Objectives

Waitpersons will learn techniques and skills to deal with Special Customer Situations. You will be better prepared to anticipate the special situations and their solutions.

Prepare yourself by reading
these readiness questions. **?**

Is it a good idea to do extras for your Customers, like giving crayons and paper to children?

What two appropriate responses are used when the Customer makes a mistaken claim about food preparation?
Can you reduce Customer problems with questions and actions?
What are the two situations appropriate to escalate to your Manager?
When do we escalate to the Chef?

✏️ *Exercise:*

Think about the extra gestures you can offer with management's support or permission. List two extra courtesies you will provide, ensuring they're backed by materials or permissions from management.

_____

_____

_____

_____

_____

_____

Extra Courtesies

Extra Courtesies are small customer-focused actions performed by most high-performance waitpersons. They include offering or providing:

Extra napkins to children or those having "messy" food.

Crayons and paper for children, end-of-meal treats if allowed by parents.

Pencils, pens and paper to business customers when you notice they are writing on napkins.

Local maps when directions are needed.

Clean silverware when needed.

To call a cab.

Scores from sporting events.

You will need to plan ahead to provide extra courtesies. Determine which courtesies will be supported by materials supplied by your management and which are permissible.

Most Waitpersons miss opportunities to do Extra Courtesies, but those who do are rewarded with increased customer ENTHUSIASM and TIPS. Your investment in any supplies not covered by your restaurant will set you above the average waitpersons and will return extra income.

Appropriate responses

"The Customer is always right" is an old adage. We know that it is not always the case. However, customers usually believe they are right. Your challenge is greatest when they are not right but believe they are Appropriate responses that accommodate customers' beliefs and perceptions rather than directly confront their assertions. When possible, adjust the order or other deliverables as if the customers are right. Realize that It is usually wiser to err on the side of the customer when possible and not too costly. Waitpersons who set about proving customers wrong receive negative results. The customer will show just how right they are by decreasing the TIPS, sometimes to nothing.

There will be some instances where the customer is wrong and must be dealt with as such. Denial of inebriation is a prime example. Recent rulings, laws and common sense require that restaurants do not continue serving inebriated customers. (Check with your management regarding this important matter).

Smoking in nonsmoking may be another case where customers are wrong and cannot be accommodated. Your appropriate responses in these cases should follow a pattern:

Courteously attempt to dissuade the customer from their actions, for example:
Offer coffee or dessert in place of liquor.
Escalate: describe the potential problem to management and indicate your level of certainty.
Follow management instructions and restaurant policy.

Most cases of "customers wrong believe they're right" will be less serious. You may tire or even feel angry when customers wrongly state:

"The food is too salty."
"This is a drafty spot."
"This city is boring."

You can use techniques to reduce your frustration:

The Physical Technique: Inhale a deep breath through your nose, then exhale slowly through your mouth. This breathing **exercise** will help to calm tightened nerves.

Recall that your income derives from your primary mission - customer satisfaction and enthusiasm.

Some comments can be ignored, but not those that relate to your service or the food quality.

Acknowledge comments with agreement, "I've heard some customers say that the city is boring.

When customers make mistakes regarding the food, remember that it is their personal taste that counts. Your appropriate response is to restate the complaint to ensure that you really understand it. Then, offer to prepare the same dish to satisfaction or offer to return with the menu for another selection.

Problems...now what?

Problems will occur on occasion, no matter how perfect your service or food is. Problems should be looked at as opportunities to demonstrate your customer focus and concern. Avoiding or immediately correcting problems will contribute to customer enthusiasm.

Problem Reducers

When customers express problems of any kind, try to resolve the problem to their satisfaction. Always restate the problem in the form of a question. For example:

"Your toast is too dark?"
"Your soup is cold?"
"Your silverware is soiled?"

After an expected "Yes" response, set expectations for a timely response by saying, for example, "I'll bring toast as you like it immediately." Remember to remove the original item from the table and replace it very quickly. You should have it the next time the customer sees you.

Sometimes, you will not know what the Customer wants you to do to correct the situation. The Appropriate Response is to restate the Customer complaint as a question. After the expected "Yes," ask your Customer

"How can I make it right for your satisfaction?"

Most Customers will tell you exactly what will make them happy under the circumstances, then tell them something like:

"I will do this immediately."

In all circumstances following satisfactory corrective action, follow up in a few minutes with questions such as:

"Is the situation now satisfactory for you?"

The follow-up will communicate that you care. Your Customers will appreciate the follow-through.

ESCALATION

When should waitpersons take customer problems to the Manager? The answer to this question is, "probably more often than most waitpersons think they should." Do not be afraid to go to the Manager for help with a customer problem or special request.

Referring a problem or request to a manager or another authority person is termed ESCALATION. The process of ESCALATION exists for the benefit of you and your customers. It can also be an opportunity for you to further understand restaurant policies.

There are two times you must escalate to your Manager for help:

A customer asks to see the Manager
You think you need the Manager's help.

Customers may ask to see your Manager for several reasons, including telling you the great job you are doing. You should attempt to determine customers' reasons to be able to prepare the Manager. Ask questions such as:

"I will be happy to get the Manager right away. What shall I tell them they can do for you?"

Regardless of the reasons, meeting customers' requests will always improve their ENTHUSIASM.

There will be times when you believe the Manager needs to help you. It may occur when you have difficult customers who complain about everything or rare abusive or rude individuals. You may even want to escalate to your Manager when serving an important party.

When you approach your Manager in such a case, say something like:

"Will you please visit my table and verify that our customer is happy?"

"Our Customer has a problem (state the problem). Will you please visit them and see what you can do to help?"

Restaurant managers are professionals dedicated to customer satisfaction. They lead a team whose function is customer enthusiasm.

Escalation to the Chef

When customers request special preparation or ask detailed questions about meal preparation, it will usually be appropriate to ESCALATE customer issues to the Chef.

You should approach Chefs with consideration and care. They are managers of food preparation and supervise numerous people. Put a request as a question, for example:

"My Customer has a special request (state the request). Can you accommodate them?"

"Our Customer has a question regarding preparation. Can you visit them?"

Chef's visits to customers are powerful statements to customers that they are important. You should review with management and Chefs when visits are appropriate.

✏️ *Exercise:*

Consider situations where it's appropriate to escalate customer issues to the chef. List two scenarios that warrant escalation.

_____

_____

_____

_____

_____

Chapter Summary

Special customer situations require good customer relations techniques, including Extra Courtesies, Appropriate Responses, Problem Reducers and Escalation.

Organize and apply the techniques to the different types of special customer situations. You will then be able to turn difficulties into increased customer enthusiasm.

Management assistance to waitpersons can be obtained via escalation. There are two types of situations when Waitpersons should escalate: a). when customers ask to see the Manager or Chef, and 2) when assistance is needed with special requests or difficult situations... You should meet with your management to determine specific escalation procedures.

Bonus Chapter: Customers are Different TYPES

This chapter is for the ELITE and Best of the Best servers who want to skyrocket their TIP income to Make More Money! A lot more!

Who are YOUR customers? How are they similar, and how are they different? Customers are the source of all revenue for Waitpersons and the entire restaurant team. But, if we only perceive customers as money providers we will fail to treat them with the warmth and individuality that they deserve.

Your objective is to help the customer have the most enjoyment possible from their dining experience. This requires a simple understanding of customer personality types and their dining reasons. You will need to adjust your service style according to the customer's personality and reason for dining.

Readiness Questions ?

Review the following as preparation for the Chapter:

How many customer personality types can you describe?
What do we call the domineering, bossy customer?
What do we call the talkative customer?
Which customer type needs a lot of information?
Which customer types need a lot of time for decisions?

CUSTOMER PERSONALITY TYPES

Your customers' personalities will determine how they make their decisions and how they communicate with you.

We can categorize customer personalities into four types:

BOSS
ENGINEER
SOCIALIZER
THINKER

B-E-S-T reminder

Remind yourself that you have only the **B-E-S-T** customers and you will be able to recall the four personality types.

BOSS customers like to be in charge and are usually very decisive and may be somewhat domineering. They want to be waited on and to control the dining experience. These personality types will want it their way right away.

The BOSS makes specific requests and frequently defines the way in which they should be handled. The Waitperson should respond to the BOSS's requests swiftly and correctly. If you are asked for something, bring it immediately. If you are unsure of what the BOSS wants, do not assume and make a mistake. Ask for clarification so that you can meet or exceed the expectations every time.

BOSS customers do not usually need a lot of detailed information. Often, the BOSS will make a decision with knowledge only of the major choices and will not need item descriptions. However, if a BOSS asks for more information about an item, it is important to take the time and answer the question very matter of factly. Do not ramble on after the information requested is supplied.

ENGINEER customers are critical analyzers of information. They require a lot of information and will evaluate choices very carefully before making a decision. ENGINEERS will want to hear about menu choices in detail and will require time to evaluate the choices before making a decision. Decisions will usually not be made without all of the facts. If you have an ENGINEER customer, ask if more time or information is needed to help make a decision. Customers who ask for special detailed meal preparations may be ENGINEER personality types. Therefore, be prepared to discuss special cooking instructions. During the FEEDING be certain to ask if specific requests were met to satisfaction.

SOCIALIZER customers like people. They are usually friendly and trusting. They frequently make decisions based on their feelings about different choices. Emotion and intuition generally guide their decision-making. Customers who ask for your recommendations will often be SOCIALIZERS. If you personally like one of the choices, make your recommendation by saying, "My personal favorite is..." or "Several customers today have remarked on their enjoyment with..." SOCIALIZERS tend to trust you, so it is very important to be honest and make recommendations based on your personal experience. SOCIALIZERS will depend on you to make things right without detailed instructions.

SOCIALIZERs are interactive customers who often want to have lively and friendly conversations with waitpersons during the Greeting and Ordering phases of the Restaurant Sales Cycle. Many Waitpersons are also SOCIALIZERS and enjoy talking with customers.

THINKERS are frequently quiet persons who will listen and observe, then think carefully about choices. The THINKER will want to reflect upon options for quite some time before making a decision. Therefore, you must give the thinker time to make decisions. Be patient and wait at the table, or give them more time by advising that you will return shortly for their choices. You can help the thinker by recommending one or two choices as Customer favorites.

The acronym B-E-S-T will help you to recall the four distinct customer personalities. It is important to remember that the four B-E-S-T personalities are general categories. Most customers are complex and have a mixture of the four personality types with one predominant. However, customers may behave as a BOSS during a business meal and as a SOCIALIZER on a social occasion. Regardless, you should vary your serving style to fit the customer's dominant personality during the sales cycle. Use the B-E-S-T customer personality profile helper, and you will more likely meet or exceed customer expectations. Customer ENTHUSIASM increases as needs and wants are met or exceeded.

 *Exercise:*

For the following customer personality types, circle Yes or No if their decisions will need a lot of information.

BOSS	Yes	No
ENGINEER	Yes	No
SOCIALIZER	Yes	No
THINKER	Yes	No

BIG BONUS CHAPTER:
Performance Indicators

Peak performance requires Excellent Waitperson skills.

Performance Indicators measure observable waitperson skills. These skills were presented throughout "Waiting Tables? Make More Money!

Consistently apply the skills to rate high on the indicators, and you will earn greater than average TIP income and Make More Money!

The performance indicators questions are:

1. Did the staff communicate with one another?

Excellent Customer Service requires teamwork. Teamwork requires effective communication. Communicate needs to your colleagues. For example, if fellow Waitpersons' tables need attention, tell them. When you need help, ask. Providing quality dining experiences is everyone's goal.

2. Did Waitperson play the "blame games"?

Self-defense is part of human nature. Therefore, we tend to blame others when something goes wrong. Many people play this "blame game," but it neither produces solutions nor improves customer enthusiasm. Quite the contrary. So, never blame another instead of seeking a solution, especially in front of Customers. You will only look worse in their eyes.

The correct action is to improve the situation. Do the best you can and seek help when needed. Examples include delays in meal preparation. Do not seek to blame the Chef. Determine if you can provide any help and convey to the customer your concern by saying, "I apologize for the delay and will try to speed things up. Meanwhile, can I get you more bread, etc.." This simple apology informs customers that you are aware of and concerned about the problem.

3. Were complaints positively handled?

Notice that we ask if complaints were positively handled. There will be complaints, some reasonable, others not. Handling complaints in a positive manner can actually increase customer ENTHUSIASM.

4. Did the Waitperson communicate effectively with customers?

Waitpersons must communicate effectively and courteously with customers. Communication consists of questions, statements, and answers.

5. Was the Good Questioning technique used?

Waitpersons must use questions to clarify customer requests and to understand complaints. Questions also let your customers know that you really want to satisfy their needs.

6. Good responding techniques used?

Responding is the action taken to a specific Customer request. Good responding includes courteously and accurately setting Customer Expectations.

7. Did the communication reflect the restaurant style?

Style refers to the restaurant atmosphere. Is it casual or formal? Does it target high-end and sophisticated dining? Your communications must match your restaurant's style. Casual settings support joking and informal language. Formal styles require more formal language and subtlety. Do not use profane language in any setting.

8. Waitperson's attitude.

It is important to have a POSITIVELY PEOPLE attitude. A POSITIVELY PEOPLE attitude makes both you and your customers feel better. They sense your good feelings about yourself and them.

9. Waitperson's problem handling.

The important thing to remember is to address every problem with prompt, effective attention. Take ownership of all problems that affect your Customer. Let them know WHAT is being done to correct the problem and WHEN it will be resolved.

10. Did the Waitperson's appearance reflect the restaurant style?

Style refers to the type of atmosphere in your restaurant. A waitperson's attire must fit the style of the restaurant. In all cases the Waitperson must have neat clothes that are clean. When uniforms are supplied, they must be clean and pressed.

11. Did the Waitperson "see and act"?

Remember the acronym D-A-N-C-E, "Do Anticipate Next Customer Expectations."

12. Was the Waitperson's sense of humor appropriate?

Waitpersons with a good and appropriately applied sense of humor convey ENTHUSIASM to their customers.

 ### *Exercise:*

First, in the chart below, rate your past Performance Indicator Skills level with an **"X."**

Next, put an **"A"** in the rating box you will achieve now that you have successfully completed.

"Waiting Tables? Make More Money!"

Perfomance Indicator	😫	🙁	😐	🙂	😁
Good Staff Communication					
Play the "Blame Game"					
Positively Handle Complaints					
Communicate Effectively with Customers					
Use Good Questioning Technique					
Use Good Responding Technique					

WRAP UP

Congratulations!

You can feel proud that your investment in "Waiting Tables? Make More Money!" will improve your Waitperson selling skills.

You are probably already enjoying increased Customer ENTHUSIASM and more TIP income.

The skills you learned should be refreshed from time to time to continue your peak performance. You can easily do this by quickly reviewing your completed **"Waiting Tables? Make More Money!"**

Wishing you much success and increased TIP income!

Please recommend **"Waiting Tables? Make More Money!"** to your fellow Waitpersons and Restaurant Managers.

Cut Laminate Review Daily

==**"TIPS come from Customer ENTHUSIASM... Period!"**==

Have a Positively People Attitude

SQAD:

Your actions are Statements,
Questions, Answers and Deliverables

TWO Minute Seating Rule:

Introduce yourself to the
customer within two minutes after seating.

Expectation Management:

ONLY reason a customer is upset --
their expectations are missed!
Manage Customer's WHAT and WHEN expectations.

Ordering Expectation Rules:

FIRST Order FAST
Special request - Pass the test!

D-A-N-C-E:

Do Anticipate Next Customer Expectations
Be Attentive

Be Accessible

GHOSTING:

Fulfill customers' needs without their awareness.

Fleeting Rule:

When customers are DONE, they are ready to RUN!

Special Customer Situations:

Extra Courtesies
Appropriate responses
Problem reducers
Escalation

B-E-S-T CUSTOMER PERSONALITY TYPES

BOSS
ENGINEER
SOCIALIZER
THINKER

www.ingramcontent.com/pod-product-compliance
Lightning Source LLC
Chambersburg PA
CBHW051551120626
46551CB00013B/1461